Six for the Road

Stephen Baker

Running time for each piece
7 minutes
Total Running time
50 minutes

TSL Drama

Published in Great Britain in 2020
By TSL (Drama) Publications, Rickmansworth
Copyright © 2020 Stephen Baker
ISBN / 978-1-913294-36-6
Cover photo: https://pixabay.com/photos/bar-pub-restaurant-rustic-barrels-406884/
Inside image: https://pixabay.com/photos/think-smile-man-hiding-enigmatic-3662455/

The right of Stephen Baker to be identified as the playwright/author of this work has been asserted by the author in accordance with the UK Copyright, Designs and Patents Act 1988.

All characters and events in this publication, other than those clearly in the public domain, are fictitious and any resemblance to actual persons, living or dead, is purely coincidental.

All rights reserved. No part of this publication may be reproduced, stored in a retrieval system or transmitted, in any form or by any means without the prior written permission of the publisher, nor be otherwise circulated in any form of binding or cover other than that in which it is published and without a similar condition being imposed on the subsequent buyer.

Rights of performance

Rights of performance for these sketches is controlled by TSL Publications (tslbooks.uk/Drama) which issues a performing licence on payment of a fee and subject to a number of conditions (specified on tslbooks.uk/Drama). The sketches are fully protected under the Copyright Laws of the British Commonwealth of Nations, the United States of America and all countries of the Berne and Universal Copyright Conventions. All rights, including stage, Motion Picture, Radio, Television, Public Reading and Translation into Foreign Languages are strictly reserved. It is an infringement of the Copyright to give any performance or public reading of any one of these sketches before the fee has been paid and the licence issued. The Royalty Fee is subject to contract and subject to variation at the sole discretion of TSL Publications. In Territories Overseas the fees quoted may not apply. A fee will be quoted on application to TSL Publications.

Contents

	page
Six for the Road	5
Generation Rock	7
The Support Worker	12
No Strings Attached	17
Women Trouble	22
The Hen Night	26
The Lock-in	31

Six for the Road

The song 'Oh What a Night' by Frankie Valli and the Four Seasons is played. Sam the barman sits on a bar stool adjacent to the bar.

Oh what a night, the last day of July 2019. A night I will always remember. I've been working here for the last two years serving the regulars and newcomers alike. Thought I'd seen everything I did, from impromptu strip shows to drunken brawls. It's surprising what drink can do to human behaviour. The more people drink, the more barriers loosen and eventually come down. Relationships unravel before your very eyes. But anyway, back to the events of 31st July. This night had everything, and I mean everything! Relationships beginning and ending, the 'one that got away' reappearing.

We'd just had a duke box put in. A lot of the regulars wanted a bit of nostalgia, live bands and singers just weren't hitting the note, if you pardon the pun. They wanted to bring back the old spirit of the pub. So we bought a duke box and the last day of July was its first night. The night started with a family get together and ended with a lock-in; and a whole lot in between. Let the story begin.

Sam walks off singing 'Oh What a Night.'

Generation Rock

Scene:
Public House

Setting:
One table, three chairs and three drinks.

Scenario:
Jim, Tony and Abi go to the local pub for a quiet family drink.

Characters:
Jim, age 67 - Abi's father and brother of Tony
casually dressed in jeans and a tee-shirt

Tony, age 59 - Abi's uncle,
in jeans and black leather bomber jacket

Abi, age 46 -
smartly dressed

Performance time:
7 minutes

Tony and Abi are sat at a table. Jim comes over from the other side of the pub.

Jim: (*Despairingly.*) I don't think much of the juke box, nothing on it pre 1990s, and who's this Ed Sheeran character?

Abi: (*Jokingly.*) I know vinyl's making a comeback, but I'm not sure if that means the 78s.

Tony: I don't know how some of these new artists make it into the charts. Some of them can only play three chords, at best. When my punk band, Tony and The Head Bangers were playing all the pub gigs, at least we managed four.

Jim: Was that between the band?

Tony: No, clever sod. All of us were capable of playing four chords. (*Tony air guitars to demonstrate.*) We were gifted.

Abi: Well, obviously not that gifted as you never got past playing in a pub. Did you? (*Sarcastically.*) I mean, you didn't get asked to open at Glastonbury, I take it?

Jim: None of these so called musicians of today or the punks in the 70s can compare with the 60's lot. We had Hendrix, The Stones and The Beatles.

Tony: (*Sarcastically.*) And Val Doonican and Ken Dodd.

Abi: I thought Ken Dodd was a comedian.

Tony: He was, it didn't stop him having a hit record. (*Laughing.*) I think Jim bought his record, queued up for hours outside the record shop he did, he didn't want to miss out.

Jim: Cheeky bugger.

Tony: The real decade for rock was the 70s, we kicked arse. Me and my band played all the gigs in Hull, the kids couldn't get enough of us. When we came off stage I was covered in spit from the audience.

Abi: Spit? (*A disgusted look on her face*). Spit? Are you sure they liked you?

Jim: That was their way of showing their appreciation. Complete head cases if you ask me.

Tony: We were an angry generation.

Abi: Angry about what?

Tony: Everything really. It was the music of the council estates, the young working class demanding to be heard.

Jim: The only problem is that you were not from a council estate and you were not working class.

Abi: My understanding is that this side of the family came from the middle class area of Hull and I've seen your school photo, you went to a grammar school. You were certainly not deprived. So what exactly where you angry about?

Jim: He didn't like the school uniform he had to wear. It made him look like a ponse.

Tony: You don't actually have to be working class to have an understanding of the struggle. I was with them all, I shared their struggle. (*He clenches his fist in the air.*) I gave them a voice.

Jim: A voice? Nobody could understand a word any of you said. You just screamed down the microphone and generally jumped up and down on the stage like a load of headcases. You were lucky some of you didn't get locked up.

Abi: Well, thankfully in the 80s we were a bit more dignified. And our generation produced Michael Jackson, George Michael and Boy George.

Jim: I wouldn't boast about that if I was you.

Tony: And what did these people ever do, except prance about in funny clothes?

Abi: Funny clothes, I've seen a photograph of you with your band and you had a Mohican haircut and your tee-shirt had great big holes in it. And as for what they did, they produced some of the best music ever.

Tony: Says who?

Abi: Says the record sales.

Tony: Record sales count for nothing, the 80s was the decade of the video. They didn't play gigs like we did, and The Clash had one of the best-selling albums ever, *London Calling*, and they never appeared on *Top of the Pops*, never mind make a video.

Abi:	Well more fool them. The problem with you two is you are stuck in the decade of your youth. I appreciate music from my youth, the 80s and through the decades. I go to Glastonbury. Which is where I'm going from here.
Jim:	You mean that place where you all wonder about in your wellington boots thick with mud, listening to someone playing some solo guitar riff for about fifteen minutes?
Tony:	I could play the lot of em off the stage. If Robbie Williams and Ed 'What's his face' each had a stage of their own and I had mine, theirs would be empty. The kids today would be blown away with my guitar playing.
Jim:	Is this your air guitar playing? Like when I caught you playing that blow up guitar in your bedroom in front of the mirror?
Tony:	I was seven years old when you all barged into my bedroom unannounced. I was practising then for the real thing. Which I knew was going to happen.
Abi:	Well, it didn't happen, did it? Anyway (*Puts her coat on.*), I'll leave you two to climb back into your Tardis. My lift has just arrived. (*Exits.*)
Jim:	Wonder who's playing this year?
Tony:	Don't know, probably some three chord wonder. I wouldn't watch them from the comfort of my armchair, never mind stand up to me bits in mud for the pleasure.
Jim:	The problem with the younger generation is they don't know a good gig when they see one. I remember coming here back in 69 when my mate Jed was booked to play a Simon and Garfunkel night.
Tony:	And?
Jim:	The place was packed. He took to the stage with his guitar. Unfortunately, he'd forgotten to bring the lyric sheet with him. (*Swigs another drink of lager from his glass.*) But he improvised. He just played the guitar.
Tony:	So it ended up a Simon without the Garfunkel session?
Jim:	Well, yeah, but we recognised the songs, it was still a good night. He still got a round of applause at the end of the night. Someone even shouted for more. So, he came back

	on and did an encore. Played a few more guitar solos from his repertoire.
Tony:	I wish some of these kids today could have seen me and my band back in the 70s. When we played this place one night, I was giving it some welly on the electric guitar and the amps exploded, the place had to be evacuated and the fire brigade called. That's what you call a gig. (*Drinks from his pint glass.*) The kids today don't know what they've missed.
Jim:	No, they certainly don't.

Ends

The Support Worker

Scene:
Public House

Setting:
One table, two chairs and two drinks.

Scenario:
A support worker meets a client in a pub. She has been allocated his case from a colleague. It is their second meeting in the same location. They sit at a table with two drinks on view. A pint glass in front of Kenneth and a half a pint glass in front of Brenda.

Characters:
Brenda, middle-aged support worker.
Attire is trendy, slim fitting jeans and a fashionable top.
Kenneth, middle-aged client.
Dressed in jeans and a tee-shirt.

Performance time:
7 minutes

Brenda: Well, Kenneth this is our second meeting at the same venue, I might add. You must like this particular pub.

Kenneth: Yes, it's okay.

Brenda: I just hope that we have an evening incident free. Unlike last week.

Kenneth: Do you mean the incident with the clairvoyant?

Brenda: Yes, Kenneth, I mean the incident with the clairvoyant.

Kenneth: I just couldn't help myself and I don't know why he's meeting clients in a pub.

Brenda: There are lots of places that clairvoyants work from and as long as the landlord has given permission, they are entitled to arrange to meet clients on the premises.

Kenneth: But, I didn't think he was a very good one.

Brenda: Maybe not Kenneth, but if the client is happy to pay whatever they have paid, then it's up to them to give an assessment of their abilities, not you, and certainly not in the manner that you did.

Kenneth: I can't really remember what I said.

Brenda: You waited for him to tell the lady he was seeing that he was a reincarnation of an Indian Chief. And you butted in by suggesting he was Big Chief Full of . . . Well anyway, let's not repeat verbatim the actual comment.

Kenneth: Oh, yes. I remember now.

Brenda: Yes, Kenneth and when the incident had been calmed down by the landlord and myself, and after I had a chat with the landlord, we agreed didn't we, Kenneth, that you would work on the issue of your abruptness.

Kenneth: Well, yes.

Brenda: There's no well yes about it, Kenneth. We did. And I had to give an assurance to the landlord that there would be no repeat of this unfortunate incident.

Kenneth: I think its turrets that makes me do it.

Brenda: Kenneth, you have been assessed whilst you were seeing your first support worker. The results came back that you do not have Tourette's. The consultant said you just need to engage brain before opening your mouth, which is something we all do Kenneth. I'm sure we would all like to speak our minds occasionally. But we don't Kenneth, we think first. You are now on your fourth support worker, which is me. The last one left with anxiety.

Kenneth: What Karen? She was unwell with anxiety?

Brenda: Yes, Kenneth she was unwell with anxiety. I am led to believe there were one or two incidents in public when you and her met, that caused her to feel anxious.

Kenneth: I can't think of any incidents. We used to meet regularly at various places and I can't think of any incidents.

Brenda: When a support worker is allocated a new client it is common practice to view the client's case notes. As I did in your case.

Kenneth: So, you've all been keeping notes on me?

Brenda: The agency keeps notes on all clients. How are we supposed to help people if we don't know the issues?

Kenneth: What issues?

Brenda: Well, in your case, Kenneth. Your rudeness. It was all the way through your notes. Every one of your previous three support workers say the same thing. That you are rude to people in the vicinity of where you meet.

Kenneth: What did Karen have to say about me? What incidents?

Brenda: Well, I seem to remember seeing something about an incident in the library café.

Kenneth: They served my sandwich with salad when I had told them I wanted it on its own. A chicken sandwich on its own. I was very specific.

Brenda: Yes, I understand you may have been specific in what you wanted. However, we all make mistakes. Sometimes wires get crossed. People don't do it on purpose. It happens to people all of the time. It's how you deal with it that matters.

Kenneth: I dealt with it very politely.

Brenda: Not according to the notes you didn't. It says you shouted at the waitress, and flung your plate up in the air, and a gentleman sitting at the next table got your salad on his lap.

Kenneth: (*Laughing*) Oh, yes I remember now. He was steaming.

Brenda: It's not a laughing matter Kenneth, it really isn't. Just think how you would have felt if that was you enjoying a nice quiet sit down after visiting the library; and you end up with a bowl of salad in your lap. You wouldn't like it, would you?

Kenneth: No, because I don't like salad, which is what caused the situation in the first place.

Brenda: Kenneth, what caused the situation wasn't the salad. It was your reaction to being served the salad. Reaction, Kenneth. Reaction.

Kenneth: It was a one off.

Brenda: It wasn't a one off, Kenneth. There was the incident when you caught a bus to go home after meeting with Jackie, who was your support worker before Karen.

Kenneth: Are you sure about an incident on a bus? I don't remember anything.

Brenda: I think Kenneth, you have selective memory. Maybe we ought to asses you for that. Jackie had set you to the bus stop. Which she didn't have to do. But she was concerned for your safety as it was a late winter evening when you had met and therefore it was dark. Jackie saw you get on the bus, and then saw the bus drive a few yards down the road, where you got off after being asked to leave by the driver, who was an Asian gentleman.

Kenneth: I think he had a cob on because he was having to work late.

Brenda: No Kenneth, he asked you to leave because when you got on the bus you informed him that you wanted to go straight home and not via Calcutta. He got very upset, and quite rightly so, and you were asked to leave the bus. Luckily, Jackie contacted the bus company in the morning and managed to defuse the situation, so the police were not involved. You were very lucky.

Kenneth: But I had to walk home. It was the last bus.

Brenda: It serves you right. It's what I've been trying to tell you since the incident last week in here with the clairvoyant. People take offence at your crass comments.

Kenneth: I can't help it. It just comes out.

Brenda: That's why we need to look at strategies. Think about what you are going to say, engage brain. Ask yourself if your comments are likely to cause offence. Think before you speak. Basically. It's common sense.

Kenneth: You mean analyse someone's reaction?

Brenda: Yes, Kenneth. Put yourself in their shoes. Ask yourself if you would like such a comment being made to you. Do you think you can do that?

Kenneth: Yes, I'm sure I can. Well, I'll give it a try.

Brenda: Good. We've made some progress, and it's only the second meet-up. Right let's have another drink to reward ourselves for addressing an important issue. I'll get them. Do you want another lager shandy? (*She points to his glass.*)

Kenneth: Yes please. And a bag of salt and vinegar crisps.

Brenda: Right. (*Gets the money out of her purse, stands up from the table and walks towards the bar.*)

Kenneth: Brenda.

Brenda: (*She returns to the table*). Yes Kenneth, have you forgotten something?

Kenneth: No. It's just that your backside don't half look big in those skinny jeans. Don't you think you should wear something more suitable for somebody of your age?

Ends

No Strings Attached

Scene:
Public House

Setting:
One table, two chairs and two drinks.

Scenario:
Two people exchange details through an advertisement in the local newspaper entitled: No Strings Attached.
They meet in a pub to arrange a sexual liaison. Both are married.
Nikki is sitting at a table and is joined by Simon.

Characters:
Nikki and *Simon*, early 30s.
Casually dressed.

Performance time:
7 minutes

Simon: I'm guessing from the description you gave me that you must be Nikki.

Nikki: (*Getting up from the table.*) You must be Simon, you look very familiar. I am sure we've met before. It wasn't in this setting because I've never done this sort of thing before.

Simon: I believe we have met before, in fact several times. We went to the same senior school. Branton High. What a coincidence. Of all the places to meet and in these circumstances. It's unbelievable. I never guessed when you answered the advert. You signed off as Nikki. When we were at school you were Nicola Johnson.

Nikki: (*Holds up her married finger.*) Now Mrs Kirk. I use Nikki now, it just sounds more modern. I see you also have a married ring on your finger. Looks like we have both found ourselves in marriages that don't fulfil.

Simon: This feels really surreal. I guess you're right about fulfilment. I'm not getting much from the relationship other than friendship. The physical side has never been great and it's diminished over the past year or so, if it was possible. I'm lucky if it's once a month. Diane just doesn't seem interested.

Nikki: Hang on a minute. You didn't marry Diane Peters from school did you? (*She laughs.*)

Simon: Well, yes as matter of fact I did. How did you guess?

Nikki: Because I remember you two going out together. I can still see you two now at the school leaving disco. She was all over you.

Simon: Yeah, well I think she was relieved that someone asked to take her to it. She wasn't my first choice.

Nikki: Diane Johnson? We all used to call her little Miss Perfect. She was a real whiz in the cookery classes. We all said she was the youngest housewife ever. She couldn't wait to get her little pinafore on and get her cakes in the oven. I bet she has your meal on the table for when you get home from work?

Simon: Well, yes she does actually. It drives me mad. She's always in the kitchen. If she's not cooking she's baking. If I set foot

Nikki:	in the kitchen she nearly batters me over the head with the rolling pin. It's like her territory. So what about you? Who are you married to and why did you answer the ad?
Nikki:	I left school and was between jobs, when I met Brian who was starting a business. He gave me a job as his personal assistant. I was swept away I guess by an older guy with ambition. He was going places. He built up his property business from nothing to a multi-million pound business. He's loaded basically. But he's extremely dull and has aged greatly in the last couple of years. He has no time for passion as he's too tired generally having worked his usual 14 hour day for 7 days a week. I hardly ever see him. All he ever says when I approach him about never seeing him is think of the luxury you've become accustomed to. I answered the ad really because I'm bored and in a funny sort of way to save my marriage. I like the lifestyle but not the person I'm with. I guess if I could have sex with someone else it might fill the void. I feel like a lost soul at times.
Simon:	Lost soul sums up my feelings really, sounds like we're in very similar situations. There's a huge void in my life that Diane just can't fill. I like her as a friend but we've just grown apart. We have no children, so there's nothing keeping us together really, but like you I feel that having casual sex may just keep the marriage together. It just hasn't happened where children are concerned. And you?
Nikki:	None. I just never felt that I wanted to bring his kids into the world. (*She takes a drink from her glass.*) I'm really intrigued about the school disco, who was your first choice, if it wasn't Miss Perfect?
Simon:	(*Drinks from his pint.*) Well actually, it was you.
Nikki:	(*Startled.*) Me?
Simon:	You must have noticed me when you were coming out of your French class? I did German. I tried to transfer over to French, so I could be in the same class as you. But I was told I had been entered for the German exam and it couldn't be changed.
Nikki:	(*Laughing.*) I think you're having me on.
Simon:	I'm not. I used to be fretting all the time I was in the German class. I would say to myself: this time I am going to

	ask her out. I would always wait near the corridor, I would see you with your friends; and would just chicken out. You never seemed to look in my direction. Then I saw you with Tom Hills. You looked like an item to me.
Nikki:	(*Laughing.*) I remember seeing you hanging around outside the classroom door. I thought you had a crush on my friend Helen.
Simon:	No. Not Helen. You.
Nikki:	Bloody hell.
Simon:	Just as a matter of interest. If I'd plucked up the courage to ask you out. What would you have said?
Nikki:	I would have said yes. I always really liked you. I envied Helen. But you didn't ask me. Then Tom did. I went out with him for about a fortnight, then I packed him in, because he was an idiot. This is really weird. We have such a shared history. Since I got married I have lost contact with all my friends from school. Brian is very controlling. He stopped me seeing all my friends, so in the end they just disappeared.
Simon:	So basically, had I been able to pluck up the courage to ask you out our lives would have been totally different. I wouldn't be going home to a housewife in a pinafore every day and you wouldn't be sat on your own in a great big house.
Nikki:	We really are lost souls.
Simon:	Indeed we are. When we corresponded by messaging, we both agreed it was going to a no-strings-attached arrangement. If you remember we agreed to meet here so we could plan out how we would meet to well, hook-up.
Nikki:	Yes we did and we were quite specific if I remember. (*Touching her wedding ring.*) Is it still what you want? A no-strings casual meet up sort of thing. I'm assuming you still fancy me or am I being presumptuous?
Simon:	No, you're not being presumptuous. I want to meet up again with the girl I idolised from afar. The girl I fell in love with. The girl I waited for in the corridor every Monday afternoon.

Nikki: (*Taking off her wedding ring.*) Simon, it might be fifteen years since we last met, but I feel something.

Simon: (*Taking his wedding ring off.*) Me too.

Nikki: There's no going back.

Simon: Don't want to.

Nikki: We make a pact here now to finish our marriages.

Simon: Agreed.

Nikki: I don't care about living in a great big house in the country.

Simon: And I don't care about Victoria sponge cakes and home-made chocolate biscuits.

Nikki: We'll be together. Living who knows where.

Simon: I don't care if we end up living on a sink basin estate in the middle of nowhere.

Nikki: I never learnt to cook you know. The best you'll get from me is a ready meal.

Simon: Sounds like bliss.

Nikki: Strange that neither of us have had children.

Simon: Maybe it just wasn't right with the people we called our partners.

Nikki: We're both in our early 30s. There's still a chance.

Simon: Well, I'll tell you what, there's no time like the present. (*Gets up from the table, and Nikki joins him.*)

Ends

Woman Trouble

Scene:
Public House

Setting:
One table, two chairs and two drinks.

Scenario:
Two friends, neighbours and work colleagues, are in a pub to discuss the marriage problems one of them is experiencing.

Characters:
John, 42
Geoff, 40
Both dressed casually.

Performance time:
7 minutes

John: Well, I tell you no one ever explains to you the difficulties you experience when you get married. When my father took me for a drink just before the wedding, all he kept saying was be prepared for the 'ups and downs.' All I can say is he should have been more specific.

Geoff: I take it you and Frances are going through a rough patch?

John: That's an understatement. It's a bloody nightmare, and I think she's got someone else.

Geoff: Well how have things got so bad?

John: Well, basically in the bed department. You see Frances let herself go a bit. When she lost her job at the shop, she had a lot more time on her hands. And all those made redundant with her were the same. So, they all started to meet regularly in the week for coffee and cake at someone's house and have a natter. You know what women are like when they get together.

Geoff: Don't forget I'm not married but I have been known to take the odd woman out. But how has this affected the bedroom activities?

John: Basically, she piled the weight on and I just didn't fancy her anymore. She went from a size 10 to a 16 in no time at all. To put it bluntly, seeing her naked was not a pretty sight. To put it succinctly, everything went south and I just didn't want to have sex with her anymore.

Geoff: That's a bit tough on the girl. You didn't tell her that did you?

John: Well, no, not in so many words.

Geoff: Not in so many words?

John: One night she came on strong, and I just told her I wasn't in the mood. She wanted to know why. Asked me if I was tired, things on my mind with work, that sort of thing. Anyway, before I knew it I blurted out I wished she was slim again; more like the girl I fancied like mad when we first met.

Geoff: Nice. I bet you got a good reaction.

John: Yes, I did. She banished me to the spare room.

Geoff: And when was that?

John: Last month.

Geoff: I take it you're still there?

John: Correct.

Geoff: But I saw Frances only last week and she looked as slim as ever.

John: Yes, I know. That leads me onto the latest problem. She went on a crash diet. Went back to a size 10. Looks gorgeous. So now I want to resume things, if you see what I mean.

Geoff: I think I get the gist.

John: But she's having none of it. She refuses all advances. She's either teaching me a lesson or she has someone else. And I think it's the latter. It's just so frustrating. It's like being in a restaurant and you can see the food being served to the next table. It looks great, you can see it but you can't taste it. I can't even have a nibble from the starter menu.

Geoff: Trust you to liken your wife to a plate of food. If she's found someone else, you can't really blame her can you? You hurt her feelings. Women want to feel wanted. No matter what. Remember your vows John, for better for worse.

John: I know that. But you can't help how you feel. It's fine a vicar giving you instructions but you can't turn your desires on like a tap.

Geoff: But to be fair John, you didn't take much notice of the vows did you? Don't forget I work with you as well as being your neighbour. You carried on seeing other women after you and Frances were married.

John: Yeah I did. Look you know the score. You've known me since I was a teenager. I played the field. I looked on marriage as driving a car. You don't suddenly slam down on the brakes, you gently squeeze them and slow down gradually.

Geoff: I think that's your way of saying you carried on jumping into bed with whoever was available and willing.

John: Well, yeah, basically. But I stopped all that by the time we'd been married a while.

Geoff: So when did the car finally stop?

John: After about two years.

Geoff: And you wonder why you've had problems in the marriage?

John: Look Geoff. Don't start lecturing me. You've been a bit of a lad yourself. Everyone knows about you and that new girl who started in admin.

Geoff: I thought you would have to bring that up. She had just broke up with her boyfriend and she needed a shoulder to cry on. She chose me, an older guy. Just to talk to. There was never anything in it.

John: Yeah, pull the other one.

Geoff: There's something I've been meaning to tell you . . . I

(*John looks towards the door and interrupts Geoff in mid-sentence.*)

John: I don't believe it. Frances has just walked in all on her own. She looks a million dollars. (*John grabs hold of Geoff's arm.*) She's eyeballed us and is coming over.

Geoff: Yes, so I see. (*Geoff looks down at his glass of lager.*)

John: She has that look of determination on her face. The same look she had when she banished me to the spare bedroom. I think she's coming over to tell me something important.

Geoff: Well, John she is joining us and we are both going to tell you something important. (*Both men look at each other.*)

Ends

The Hen Night

Scene:
Public House

Setting:
One table, three chairs and three drinks.

Scenario:
Three work friends go to a pub for a hen night. One of them is the bride to be. They are early. Others will be joining them later. They have all had a little too much drink. All three have a drink in front of them. Music is playing in the background throughout.

Characters:
Meghan, age 19 - has an 'L' plate hung around her neck
Linda, age 31
Gina, age 52, thrice divorced
All three are dressed smartly for a special night out.

Performance time:
7 minutes

Gina: It's good we've agreed to meet before the rest come. It'll give us a chance to talk before everyone gets drunk and starts talking bollocks. You know how it gets when girls hit the town.

Linda: Well this time next week Meghan you'll be a married woman. It'll be Mrs Davies.

Meghan: (*Sentimentally.*) Yeah, I know. I can't wait.

Gina: Yes, it's your last few days of freedom. So make the most of them.

Linda: Don't put it like that. You'll put her off. You make it sound like she's getting a jail sentence.

Gina: That's because she is.

Meghan: I'm really looking forward to marrying Matt. We are meant for each other. (*She swoons.*) I can't wait for those cosy night-ins lying on the sofa watching television.

Gina: Well, you just make sure you get the TV remote and put your name on it. Let him know who's in charge of the TV. That's your property. You decide what you watch not him. He'll have football on every night if you let him.

Meghan: You make it sound like a war of attrition not a marriage.

Linda: Don't take any notice of her Meghan. She's been married and divorced three times. She's practically got a season pass for the divorce courts. If you follow her advice hubby will be filing for divorce before you've had chance to digest your wedding cake.

Gina: Meghan's a little green if you ask me, and I think she would benefit from someone, who, shall we say, has been around the track a few times.

Linda: Been around track a few times? You've just about lapped everyone else in the race.

Gina: I count myself a bit of an expert on men. It'll be good for Meghan to listen.

Linda: Been married three times doesn't make you an expert. You might have been the problem.

Meghan: Hello. I'm still here. (*She says exasperated.*)

Linda: Maybe Meghan would be better listening to me. Me and Ken have been happily married for ten years. It's give and take. If Ken wants to watch sport on the TV, it's fine. I just take myself off to the back room and watch what I want to watch on the television in there. Or I read a book.

Gina: So you throw the towel in.

Linda: No Gina, it's a compromise.

Meghan: (*Totally exasperated.*) I'm not claiming ownership of the remote. And that's that. We have bought everything together and we will share everything together.

Gina: Men never share anything. Well, unless they've caught something nasty down below. They'll share that with you.

Meghan: My Matt wouldn't do such a thing. (*Getting upset.*)

Linda: I think Gina is referring to her first husband, who, shall we say, liked women.

Gina: Liked them! He couldn't get enough of them. When I told the family I was getting married, father asked if it was a shotgun wedding. (*Turning to look at Meghan.*) That's pregnant, Meghan. Then mother took me to one side and told me how difficult married life would be. Then she warned me of the seven year itch. I didn't know she meant literally. Took weeks of treatment to get rid of the symptoms. I've never been so embarrassed and if things couldn't possibly get any worse, the woman down the street worked in the VD clinic. I never knew where to look when I was out doing my shopping and she seemed to appear from nowhere.

Meghan: I'll have you know my Matt is loving and caring.

Gina: Well, just make sure you keep an eye on him. Make sure it's just you he's loving and caring to.

Linda: I'm sure Meghan knows her own mind, and knows and trusts Matt. I've met him, he seems a really nice lad.

Gina: I thought I knew my own mind when I met Dan.

Linda: Husband number one.

Gina: Then after he was despatched, I met Tom.

Linda: Husband number two.

Gina: Yes, alright Linda. You're not John Motson. We don't need a running commentary on affairs. I'm just trying to help the girl. Yes, I've met Matt, and yes, he seems a nice lad. But you just never know.

Linda: I'm sure Meghan and Matt will have many happy years together. (*She raises her glass and stands on her chair.*) Here's a toast to Meghan and Matt. May they live happily ever after.

Gina: You make it sound like a fairy story. But anyway, cheers. (*Takes a drink from her glass.*)

Meghan: To me and Matt. (*Takes a drink from her glass.*)

Gina: I'm assuming the train has already visited the tunnel.

Meghan: Sorry, what train and what tunnel? Matt had a train set when he was a young boy. But he's done with all that now he's a man.

Linda: I think she's referring to sex.

Meghan: Well what about it?

Gina: Take my advice. Only do it when you want to and on your terms. None of this just a quickie, I'm up early in the morning palaver. If he's wants it, make sure he puts maximum effort into it, or he gets nothing at all.

Meghan: I'm entering a marriage contract, not signing an agreement. We discuss everything before we do anything. We're a real couple.

Gina: And what about the house? Is it in your name?

Meghan: (*Getting flustered.*) Yes, I mean no. It's a joint mortgage.

Gina: Have you signed a pre-nuptial?

Meghan: A pre whater?

Linda: Gina you're practically interrogating the poor girl. Give her a break.

Gina: I'm just trying to make sure that if things go wrong, she doesn't end up out on the streets.

Meghan: Out on the streets? My Matt would never do that to me.

Linda: Meghan, just calm down. I'm sure everything will be just fine.

Gina: I'm sure it will. But always best to be on the safe side. Check the mortgage application on the house when you get home. That's all I'm saying.

Meghan: *(Totally flustered.)* I have no intention of doing any such thing. Marriage is based on trust. I'm going to be a wife, not an MI5 agent.

Linda: You're unsettling the girl.

Gina: All I'm doing is trying to protect her. Now Meghan, I've seen you both out walking your dogs. Are they a bitch and a dog?

Meghan: Well, yes. Of course. That's what couples do. They always get one of each.

Gina: Well you just make sure you get the male. If things go wrong you don't want to be stuck with a bitch dropping a litter like it's going out of fashion. It'll cost you a fortune.

Linda: Gina you've gone too far.

Meghan: *(Sounding upset.)* Me and Matt love both dogs exactly the same.

Linda: Stop it Gina.

Gina: Make sure you get him to make out a Will leaving everything to you. You don't want some slapper coming from nowhere and taking everything you've worked for.

Meghan: I've a good mind to call the whole thing off. *(Bursts into tears and runs off to the toilet. The song 'Chapel of Love' by the Dixie Cups can be heard in the background.)*

Linda: *(Getting up from her seat.)* Gina, you've really done it now.

Gina: Well that's the younger generation for you. They think they know everything and never want to listen to good advice. *(Takes another drink from her glass.)* Next thing you know they're crying for help. I just despair with them. I really do.

Ends

The Lock-In

Happy Anniversary, Darling

Scene:
Public House

Setting:
One table, two chairs and two drinks.

Scenario:
Sam and Helen and have been married for ten years. They sit at a table in a Public House.

Characters:
Helen, 50s
wearing a lovely dress

Sam, 50s
in jeans and a casual shirt.

Performance time:
7 minutes

Helen: Well, it's really romantic of you to bring me to the local pub on our anniversary Sam; and to boot to arrange with your mate the landlord to have a lock-in after hours.

Sam: (*Taking a drink from his pint glass.*) Don't mention it darling, it was the least I could do.

Helen: Other women get breakfast in bed, some flowers and a bit of romance. I get a drink after hours at the Nags Head.

Sam: I thought you'd like the atmosphere. You need to soak it up.

Helen: Soak it up. There's every dodgy person in the area all in the same place. If the police did a raid they'd solve most of the crime in the area in one fell swoop.

Sam: Relax. Everything is above board.

Helen: It's not above board at all. That's why they call it a lock-in. We are drinking after hours with the pub doors locked. So the police don't come in. We are breaking the law.

Sam: No one will know.

Helen: You are forgetting one very important fact Sam. I'm a school teacher. I'm supposed to be a pillar of the community. I teach children right from wrong.

Sam: And your point is?

Helen: My point is, parents of some of the children are in the pub. One guy over there near the juke box hasn't taken his eyes off me since we got in here. I thought I recognised him. It's Sarah Wilson's dad. I had to lecture her in front of him about stealing from the school kitchen.

Sam: He's hardly going to say anything, is he? When he shouldn't be in here himself.

Helen: Why can't you be like other blokes? Rachel's hubby Terry whisked her off to Paris for the weekend for their tenth anniversary. You bring me to the Nags Head.

Sam: If it's romance you want, I can see what's on the juke box. Maybe some Demis Roussos? Or Barry White?

Helen: I don't want to listen to Demis Roussos or Barry White. I want to be whisked away to somewhere nice and romantic. Where the people are pleasant and drink wine, not beer bellied guys guzzling pints of lager down their throat like there's no tomorrow.

Sam: I take it you're not totally happy with the venue?

Helen: How very observant of you. You're obviously content with the venue, you spend most of your life in here.

Sam: I think that's a bit of an exaggeration. I come here for a quiet drink with the lads on a Sunday afternoon to watch the footie.

Helen: Yes, so you do. Only thing is Sam, you're forgetting how observant I am, a typical teacher never misses a trick as you always say. The football on a Sunday is on Sky. Correct?

Sam: Correct.

Helen: So, where are the Sky posters advertising the matches? We are right in the middle of the football season and no posters are up informing of upcoming games. Funny that.

Sam: Ah, well you see, it's just word of mouth. The regulars don't need posters to tell us what's on. We just know.

Helen: I'm sure you do. But obviously for some events you do need a poster to remind you of what's on.

Sam: Come again?

Helen: I wish I could.

Sam: Don't get onto that again. This is neither the time nor the place.

Helen: On the wall adjacent to the men's toilet is a poster. (*She points over to the wall.*) There, do you see it? That poster tells us what is really going on here on a Sunday afternoon. Strippers! The poster says: Every Sunday afternoon a selection of strippers.

Sam: Ah, well yes, in the bar maybe. Not in the lounge where we are. Shall I get you another drink? Another half a lager with lime?

Helen: No, I do not want another lager and lime, thank you very much. You've been lying to me for months. All the time I've been working in the house on a Sunday afternoon, you've been ogling other women. Naked! Haven't you?

Sam: Well, yes, but . . .

Helen:	Never mind but. And what have you been doing as regards the physical side to this so called relationship?
Sam:	You know what I've been doing. I have been visiting the chemist for the 'magic blue' tablets.
Helen:	Ah, yes the magic blue tablets. That you forget to take half the time. Did you think about taking one last night maybe, so we could celebrate our anniversary in style?
Sam:	Well, no, but I took one just before we came out tonight, and it's starting to work.
Helen:	(*Gets hold of her coat and starts to put it on.*) Right, well we had better get home pretty sharpish, before it wears off.
Sam:	I better see the landlord.
Helen:	What do you mean see the bloody landlord. What the hell for?
Sam:	Because it's a lock-in and he's got the keys.
Helen:	(*Sternly.*) Well go and find him. Like yesterday.

(*Sam gets up from his seat and walks to the bar, he returns a minutes later.*)

Helen:	Well?
John:	The bar staff don't know where he is.
Helen:	What do you mean they don't know where he is? (*Raising her voice.*) It's his bloody pub.
Sam:	He and one of the barmaids disappeared about ten minutes ago. One of staff said come back in about twenty minutes.
Helen:	Twenty minutes. Well, I can tell you this is going to be the longest twenty minutes of your life, Samuel Kirby. (*She folds her arms aggressively.*)
Sam:	I always knew when I was in trouble when I was a kid. My mother referred to me by my full name.
Helen:	Trouble? You don't know what trouble means. (*She slumps in her chair with her arms folded.*) If Private Thomas isn't stood to attention when we get home, your life won't be worth living.

Ends

www.ingramcontent.com/pod-product-compliance
Lightning Source LLC
Chambersburg PA
CBHW071804040426
42446CB00012B/2698